The Medicine Wheel

Also by Adrian Rogers and published by Ginninderra Press
The Sun Behind the Sun
Between Two Hemispheres
The Prisoner's Messenger
Seasons, Situations and Symbols (Pocket Poets)
Human Nature & the Welfare State (Pocket Polemics)
Croagh Patrick (Pocket Places)
Port Victoria (Pocket Places)

Adrian Rogers

The Medicine Wheel

The Medicine Wheel
ISBN 978 1 76041 456 6
Copyright © text Adrian Rogers 2017
Cover image: Adityamadhav83 (Own work) [CC BY-SA 3.0
(https://creativecommons.org/licenses/by-sa/3.0)],
via Wikimedia Commons

First published 2017 by
GINNINDERRA PRESS
PO Box 3461 Port Adelaide 5015 Australia
www.ginninderrapress.com.au

Contents

Prelude	7
The Medicine Wheel	9
Part 1 Turning, autumn to winter	11
On the Cusp – Prelude	13
Kakadu – Midday Dancers	14
When the stars come out	15
El Greco Recounts His Dreaming	16
Autumn Adagietto	17
Light…	18
Part 2 Turning, winter to spring	19
On the Cusp – Magical Chemistry	21
The Scapegoat – Holman Hunt's Confession	22
Refugee Witness	23
Anzac Day – Dawn Service	24
Anzac Day – the Parade	25
Mary Magdalene and the Wheel	26
Part 3 Turning, spring to summer	27
On the Cusp – Rhapsody	29
The Enigma – Who am I?	30
The Albatross and the Voyager	32
Dietrich – One Man's Conscience	33
The Universal Spiral	34
Forget-me-not – separated by persecution	35
Part 4 Turning, summer to autumn	37
On the Cusp – A Reflection	39
J.G. – In Memory	40
Frost Web	41
To the Desert – A Pilgrimage	42
Rough Seas	43
Autumn is an Elegiac Melody	44

Part 5 Turning, the Cathars' Equinox 1244	45
Montsegur's Speaking Dead	47
Voices in the Wind	48
The Stone and the Matrix, 1244	49
The Cathar	50
Question and Answer	51
The Witness Speaks Again	53
Unfinished Symphony; Reprise	54
Part 6 Turning, at the Zenith	57
On the Cusp of the Solar Meridian	59
Southern Hemisphere Winter Green	60
The Castaway	61
The Ocean and the Soul	62
Voss – the Enigma	63
Part 7 Turning, From Night to Dawn	65
On the Cusp – Night Into Dawn	67
Sailing Alone – in Memoriam, Joshua Slocum	68
What a Joke	69
Columba – Dove of the North	70
The Alchemy of Overcoming	72
Change – Schizophrenic	73
Part 8 Turning, to a Modern Dreamtime	75
On the Cusp of Dreaming	77
Mangrove Swamp Evocation	78
At the Old Year's Edge	79
Aftermaths of Celebration	81
Early Youth – Chasing Buses	82
Two Breaths	83
…and in Conclusion	85
Rembrandt's Vision	87

Prelude

The Medicine Wheel

Good medicine
for the heart's disclosure
is an Emmaus road
after peripheral separation
where the centre holds
for all and one
prince and pauper
a lifelong thread
drawing one and all
into the supremely knowing

the stop/start, turning
Medicine Wheel's
evolving instability
is lightning touch
charged, burning
past-future continuities
in the darts of gnosis
and a constellation's
daisy chain like unities
uncurtaining the dark
to reach the light.

Part 1

Turning, autumn to winter

On the Cusp – Prelude

A ragged pause
at the leaf fall end
on the cusp
of autumn and winter

storms die
earth voices call no longer
and winter's onset
anaesthetises remnant living
land/water essences
under luminously shaded
fluctuating skies

leaves no longer
helter-skelter swept
airborne every way
or tossed on river runs
when migrant waders leave
the shallows undisturbed
their songlike calls unsung.

Tricoloured seasons
held the trees in fief
between light, dark,
cold and heat
leaving no time for grief
only a brooding
silence of transition
foreshadowing winter's coma
and over-earth's-curve
distant, spring's returning.

Kakadu – Midday Dancers

Rock faces day-long amplify
contact points
touch repelling intrusions
of heat attacking waves
rejecting shimmering
mirage confusions

rock-painted figures
stone stage ballets
dancing through
heat-veiled orchestrations
line-limned
vibrantly alive
until the setting sun's
swift sinking coda
uplifting heat into itself
snap cools rocks
and long-hot iron roofs.

When the stars come out

Night time cooling
an earth/stone oven plate
shrink-stresses rock
into chilled apathy
as darkness supervenes
its shape deluding canopy
and stars pay court
before Orion's outline
sharply jewelled
a coldly bright display
zenith-soaring
his upraised club
a cosmic Pharaoh's
irresistible challenge
to a riven created order

yet here is no game
to hunt the Emu in the Sky
engrail another sacrifice
upon the Southern Cross,
his destiny forever set
crosses the blackness
pulsating gold and white
a ceremonial
night-long retrocession.

El Greco Recounts His Dreaming

Light across stone deceives the eye
paling or yellowing weathered grey
creating enigmas
of substance and shadow
where a mind wanders
cobbles disturb tired feet
and stinks from narrow lanes
rise round me

astigmatic vision
alone sees One
among the olive trees
in night-long pain
gazing transcendent
with such unfettered love
as turns the world of senses
to futility
disabling me thereafter
from painting amid shadows.

The darkness is consciously
winter dreaming
with my heart aflame
and the night illumined
by inner light.

Autumn Adagietto

Still day leaf falls
rust red twist and flutter
across barred light and shadow
a stretched, rhapsodic dream
like Mahler's Adagietto
drifting strings and harp
timed freely, chordal,
stretched-out, slowly
unheeding the sacrifice
a hemisphere away
of foot broken bark
angular branches
like pained affirmations
and clinging leaves
matt-polished, pinched
yet life affirming

only the autumn light
across separated seasons
shares pale, bright-edged
clarity and poise.

Light…

invisible
is darkness visible
to be
beyond comparison
rested upon, until
the Morning Star
illuminates
long rays cast
towards the spiral
compressing light
into enlightenment's
resurrection from
the passage grave
of self.

Part 2

Turning, winter to spring

On the Cusp – Magical Chemistry

Between branch, leaf,
and two breaths
peripheral vision
catches a miracle
small deaths defeated
and ley lines channelling
resurrection along
the sun's path returning
from dark time winter's
shortest day
as the kernel at last
breaks open
revealing life within.

Eternally rhyming
green versus green
and blossoming fantasias
transiently cascading
into spring's pictorial
new hung gallery
turn back on grief
when hope has hitched
a ride on Phaeton's
gold-winged chariot.

No 'Ave Caesar!'
stops the long wave's
equinoctial inrush
or the graves
from bursting open
to loosen Venus' girdle
for love, birth, and spring.

The Scapegoat – Holman Hunt's Confession

A dune wave lifts
against sun white burning
as if hammering heat
would ignite the ground
beneath cloven feet.

A scapegoat burdened
beyond hot sand over stone
by stretched out centuries
descends
through thirst, hunger,
motiveless and outcast
towards a merciless barrier
bearing evil's
outdrawn transmission
never to know
if cool oases glimmer
beyond that treacherous
shape changing bulk because
He, of two goats drawn by lot
is chosen, while I
in the backwash of trawled years
paint defencelessness
as priestly piety
offloads conscience
onto custom.

Refugee Witness

We are
internationally embarrassing
travelling people
in flight from burnings
the leavings
of politics, wars,
and western democracy.

Beyond seasonal greetings
unbar your soul's doors,
shake not the dust
of our presences
off spotless garments
for we threaten
no customary theocracy
trekking anyway, anyhow,
pilgrims regressing
from bombed-out dreams
schemes
and ambitions of conquest,
seekers
voiceless speakers
seeking only

'a place to call home.'

Anzac Day – Dawn Service

They stand like sentinels
blacker than night
awaiting a bugle's
lonely metallic voice
sprung back echoes
from the paling dark
of a pre-dawn sky
above bowed heads

echoes dying
as the sun probes
flinging a light fan
over cut-sharp edged
black horizon curves
while behind them
a small town sleeps.

Anzac Day – the Parade

Day stretches itself
along main street
a long light funnel
for marchers swinging
into drill poised lines
their march/play
well rehearsed

mark-timers from
polished instruments
brass-blown sun catchers
sounding so easily
memorialising
across time, bridging
the generational divide.

Mary Magdalene and the Wheel

The Wheel of Fortune did her no favours
when she broke the alabaster jar
releasing perfume overpowering
for love

extravagance, a sour note
the only comment
regarding treasure
brought so expensively
by caravan from India
across hard and dusty
bandit threatened miles
for what; a wedding,
burial, to sabotage
the customary?

Love, on the vine
unwithering could only
from such rootstock rise
to leaf, bud, flowering, fruiting,
intertwining
beyond autumnal fall
and winter desolation's
passing hours, days, months,
the business ledger
of uncounted years
outrunning time
on the road to eternity.

Part 3

Turning, spring to summer

On the Cusp – Rhapsody

New life's brief love affair
abounding multi-green
pink/white dot showered
fuelled by desire's thrust
hoodwinks Eros
into unrelenting dreams
of permanence
before late spring
on the summer's cusp
shrugs off her
jacaranda blue displays
and gold-flame candled
silky oaks,
pulse slowed from love's
first leaf green, bud,
and flowering fickleness.

Riverine and reservoir
levels falling
forebode tongue-tasting
summer dryness
slowing, but unfailingly
sun ruled
green darkening
foreshadowing
time's distance closing
multiple fruition.

The Enigma – Who am I?

I am the Fool
with a dog at his heels
a troubadour, a bard,
a minstrel's song
on the long and winding road
to summer
I am love cool
then fire hot.

The wheels of time
turn relentlessly
and lore, hard
on a stretching mind
is long in reach
a goad in all seasons,
and this, my alchemy's
rhyming transformation
holds the key
opening a strong door.

I am
'The Nightingale and the Rose'
the perennial philosophy
love that glows
like the stars
stronger than gods
and demons,
the way of the heart

a sacred way
spring for the knower
in temple rites
'the dayspring from on high'
a promise;

who am I?

The Albatross and the Voyager

The albatross
sweep-scanning
between sky and ocean
questing immortality
surfs scud-flying
foam-slicked wave crests
for a mariner
grave and stalwart,
his sails the wind song's
sounding chambers
under grey-cold
vastly sombre skies
uncompromising
spellbinding him
on the edge
of elemental being
divorced
from social sustenance
alone, and called
unceasingly

'Beyond the horizon's
tipping point self-launch
into the Void
touch the stars.'

Dietrich – One Man's Conscience

Rise and fall
conscience and consciousness
activating is
the heel snapping dog
emerging
humanity coming of age
rejecting the crooked
for the straight when
the Judge stands at the door,
'a cloud of witnesses'
an oratorical call
beyond altar and market place
a closed gate
chequered floor
sunset, sunrise, glamour,
a roar of wildness from the heart
and no surrender
before opening trapdoors
loosing prophetic warnings
finding the hidden word
in the detritus of desire.

'Against the prison wall
facing black fire's
travesty of justice I pass
through darkness into light.'

The Universal Spiral

White stone walls
entrance and passageway
do not enchain the spirit
light reflecting
from the caduceus
DNA
the universal spiral
at its heart.

Forget-me-not – separated by persecution

I saw him, on a station platform
withdrawn but alert, attentive,
an upraised hand
a small blue jewel-flash
a forget-me-not was set into his ring.

The stranger spoke, not the norm
surely, such sudden impulsive
knowing but the band
of brotherhood, a dash
of illumination making the heart sing.

'Brother, sister, anywhere,
remember the Chain-of-Union?

'A daisy chain ran round our temple walls
for we lived always in the day's eye
until they broke the guarded door
and cast us out
beyond the world's fair places.
Clasp hands with me
and may we meet in better times
when light breaks through the darkness
once again.'

A train rolled in. Touch was warm
between us, then he left, incisive
but gentle, yet no crash
of slamming doors could mask the sting,
that sense of loss.

'Brother, sister, anywhere
remember the Chain-of-Union
and may we meet again in light,
love's circle completed…

till then, forget-me-not.'

Part 4

Turning, summer to autumn

On the Cusp – A Reflection

A cusp's balance shift,
summer's rearguard action
against autumn's drift
tide-like north or south
as hemispheres determine
is bees droning
a passing threnody

autumnal limitations
and sun power cooled
for fruiting
shortening days
bark splitting underfoot
wind austerely chilled
on tongue and lips

autumn hassling
remnant summer stragglers
into memory's strongroom
raining after dryness
blowing after calmness.

Dried grass
and grey/green enduring
eucalyptus leaves dancing
with red-gold rusted
deciduous partners
seek a mutual relief
mist cooled by masquerades
shrouding the ritual way
of summer's requiem.

J.G. – In Memory

You walk among us no longer
neither footsteps
missteps
passing in and out of time
pacing
the eternally gold-ringing
circumpolar stars
luminous beyond shadow
cutting the rhyme
of rhythmic presence
stronger
than before side-stepping
into light,
dispelling dark moments
leaving
some store of love
on life's foreshore
for our passage of that sea
between time and eternity's
interaction;

we await your greeting
on the farther shore.

Frost Web

Temporary magic
lawn white
a spider's web crystalline
sacred geometry
a thin bright
sun-cold burning
silver-etched stillness
is transitory timelessness.

To the Desert – A Pilgrimage

Iron shod staff,
an insightful progression
from bitumen, stone and concrete
trains consciousness
to apperceive the true
in a time-deserted sanctuary
Tanami, the Archetype

'a little learning is a dangerous thing'
discretely age related to an inner self
aware of spirit lack
an inability to share
acquired, back to basics
intuited knowledge
but come awake to light,
colour, blended earth
air and sound-scapes
privileged to see
through heat shake
and shimmer bright
unpretentious outlines
and whatever shines
where not a ledge breaks
solemnity's flat line understated
and revelations
of unrecorded lives imprinting
earthed, ethnic memories.

Rough Seas

A lead grey sea's
shoreline white disintegration
advances
ominous after long retreats
from summer beaches
when withdrawal
was the daily aftermath
of tidal running

a water singing
rough-chorused drag
across pebbled slopes
cold charges inundations
obliterating hot-toned memory's
slow enchanted days.

Autumn is an Elegiac Melody

Autumn is my forest past
a leaf choked gutter in the present
'a time, times, and half a time'
the last place corralled by memory,
debris swept on river runs
washed clean of grime
drifting, rootless

recollections blurred
elusive images starring
a hemisphere away
in the specious brevity
of coolly felt intrusions
sharply brittle with fallen
dust exuding bark
stark, chilled air, rain
on eucalyptus leaves
tanged by menthol and wet wood

only shortened days
abruptly stinging showers
skies imprinted
by flights of migrant birds
and fleeting, timely recollections
link them timelessly.

Part 5

Turning, the Cathars' Equinox 1244

Montsegur's Speaking Dead

Autumn fires the lower slopes
bracken rust-red
across grass-pale green
cutting off
where grey rock scree
spills randomly
encircling bone bare
wind-torn heights.

Ruined stone walls
fusing rock surfaces
raise broken-topped barriers
mute witnesses
supplicating a world
passing below on new-made roads
as if the past no longer spoke

yet the dead speak
across wall-cast shadows
in voices of wind-riding birds
circling coldly eroded battlements
through sun, rain and
winter snow whisperings
among nooks and crannies.

Voices in the Wind

'We plead with you to meet us
in the winter of our searching
for the stone-hard way
of reconciliation
and ultimate returning
when the laurel will be green again
after seven hundred years.'

The Stone and the Matrix, 1244

Seasons are undifferentiated
to a rough-edged stone
grey-splintered from a wall
to almost insignificance
by wind and rain born centuries
except for half heard echoes,
stirrings in the Matrix
uneven coolness
timeworn smooth
compressing evocations

soundings
head ringing, echoing,
circling, aware, haunting
the seen and unseen
energies fixated
by the speaking dead
screened from its regard
while this stone, bonded
with a mountain castle
silver cloud and star encircled
above precipitous slopes
challenges the race
of temporal seasons
serving, like the Grail
the Fisher King's defiance
of clerical conspiracies
in the space-time continuum.

The Cathar

A sun-shadow mantled dreamscape
looms between fractured peaks

a black-robed, pale-faced,
unassuming stranger
paces a stony path
carrying, hung from the neck
a gospel leather bound
gaze outward turned
towards the heights
but not exclusively
because he too would know
if that stone, mortared
with its coldly plumb-line
regulated kind once
shielded the guardians
of a universal Grail.

Confusion's countermanding
wind-born voices
of Montsegur's defenders
footsteps muted or stilled
sound-smothering fear
against wall-breaking
catapulted stones
separating one from its kind
unknowingly linking across
bleakly desperate centuries
twelve thousand spaced-out
miles, speechlessly destined
to awakening.

Question and Answer

'To what force
can one stone bare witness
after seven hundred barren years;
the Matrix' powers to turn
prophesying truth
to indemnifying defeat
for freethinkers destined
by branding's desensitising
to the judgement of specious lies?'

'My voice age-hollowed
will not tell all the heart knows
but let the defendants
hold court for their day
and the stone speak
one last time
for two hundred steadfast Cathars
with their loyal friends
walking the downward path
one last time
witnessing their backward looks
one last time
towards battered walls risen grey
against a morning-pale sky
one last time
before hunch-shouldered slopes
sheltering late snow patches
hid them from view
one last time
journeying to the fires below

'watching still as smoke rolled back
towards stone crowned heights
one   last   time'

The Witness Speaks Again

His voice, crescendo and
diminuendo, age-long distorted
by propaganda moulded into
history was still articulate to
commandeer responsiveness
with evening closing in upon
a commonality of heart and mind;

'My brother dead, returned
and living still, the uncomplaining
brave I knew refused to ratify
a rotten compact between
Church and State,
challenging the Matrix'
spurious proclamation
that terrorising forces merely
with some collateral damage
policed the innocent.

'Instead, the "Perfect" chose
firstborn and comers late
a marriage to eternity,
making the Matrix powerless
to stay committed ones from
quitting a contemptible illusion
because they saw, within the fire
a gateway to the infinite
one last time.'

Unfinished Symphony; Reprise

His rite of passage
merged with night's onset
mantling soaring peaks
the half-hidden road to Tabor's
caves of final refuge
and now, in the age's cusp
this stone turns in my hand
one   last   time

ratifying
diversely tongued
crescendos of lost voices
binding
the Matrix' powers
with words like manacles
finding
earth irrefutably aligning
with suns into the Centre
grinding
established dogmas down
until their stark progenitors
haunt the broken walls
of star-born Montsegur
clustering
around its overshadowing
memories

'We plead with you to meet us
in the winter of our searching
for the stone-hard way
of reconciliation
and ultimate returning,
when the laurel will be green again
after seven   hundred   years.'

Part 6

Turning, at the Zenith

On the Cusp of the Solar Meridian

A blazing
meridian-white explosion
obliterating blue
from centre to horizon
fires from the zenith
life erasing close-quartered

weaponry of mass destruction
beneath solar chariot axles
life creating
and sustaining by distance
is stone-speak
the Sphinx's riddle
touch, pain and illumination.

Creatures curse this power
civilisation
is a weapon of mass distraction.

Chariot halting
war not over
is judgement distributed equally
wheels within wheels
moving
at the Warden's command

a meridian passes.

Southern Hemisphere Winter Green

Winter green overruns out-flush
summer-beige islands of drought
softening sinuous branches
and dark-shaded eucalyptus leaves
enhancing a magpie's
brief rippling sung melisma
floating cold/clear under cloud
while water for the river
plays a waiting game.

The Castaway

A ship under sail swing/sways
wind and wave adapting
from time divorced
deferring
one thousand miles from land
to elemental interplays
referencing the sea's judgement

on a distant shore
slow days long-stranded
sun scorched
infer endless hopes
deferring, waiting
on a sky painting sail
colouring the horizon line
with eyes hand-shaded
aching against the light.

'Hope deferred maketh the heart sick'
on shores hot-sanded
annealing a castaway
skin as though torched
still persevering
in hope of rescue
with one sail ending
time's perversity.

The Ocean and the Soul

No disconnect
between the ocean and the soul
an enharmonic variance
draws both within
a cosmic, dragon-like
free flowing raga
pulsating through reversing
tides of consciousness
inflected, musically modulating
side-slipping, echoing
like change rung bells tolling
unplumbed being's depths
uplifted by the ocean's
interwoven voices singing
a becoming to the stars
as one.

Voss – the Enigma

In burnt light red heart country
sun flashings spark
off scattered stones,
transitory stars dropped
into heat amid
meridian disguising mirages
defied by twisted, sinuous
exhausted shrubs
grey-green and racked
by root-bending droughts
lethargically awaiting
sunsets colour changing
haze emergent humps
and weathered hills
scarcely conceiving
caught in this enigmatic
midday furnace

of distant coastlines
fringed by dark green
rainforest extravaganzas
living beyond dreaming
like a decorative dress hem.

On red centre and green edge
foresightedness intuited
exploration's impact
antithetical to otherness
neither Europe, Asia,
America or elsewhere,
until his passing
into an old land's heart.

Part 7

Turning, From Night to Dawn

On the Cusp – Night Into Dawn

False dawn
is a luminously
subtly grey illusion
distantly paling
when outcomes for day
undecided
imaginatively saunter
through moments
confluences, images
half revelations
and hardening shapes
emerging into colours
lightly elevating
unreal into real.

Storm, calm,
sun or cloud overhanging
in and out breaths
cluster, from times forgotten
silently broken
by earth-sky chanting
the Morning Star down
into dawn's choral raising.

Sailing Alone – in Memoriam, Joshua Slocum

Wave lift and slate-dark sky
were more than insignificance
or otherness
in world encircling
solitary ocean wanderings
beyond ice blink
and fast, wild thundering
global-racing waves
watched over
by albatross ghost-gliders
through pioneering moments

surf-skimming long-sloping rollers
as a lonely revelation opened
on the cusp of living
under coldly dark
and stark spell-bindings.

Sextant, compass,
and dead reckoning
displayed the elemental lore
of sailing's mastery for one man
until his passing into
the ineffable Great Silence
course set beyond
storm-bound necessity.

What a Joke

They think they know you
but the real 'you'
being eternally
behind the smile
like a jewel
enclosed in its case
is gold
and shining diamond
unseen
for what it is.

Columba – Dove of the North

I trod the path of prophecy
in Aries
before the Wheel of Fortune
spun me into Pisces
awakening
under pearl-bright dawns
to hard edged tribal loyalties
conflicted loves
exile enforced from Erin
Derry my sacred oak grove
and stone-faced oratory.

I, Dove of the North
tamed the flesh
for secrets long remembered
treasures buried
half forgotten, sleeping,
hemmed in
by granite walls, guarded
by horns of light
in a rock-bound island's
green-gemmed heart

secrets held
for revelation in the cusp
of yet another age
when the crucible of change
bloodline blending
with the Porphyry Stone
will break the seal.

'Nothing is lacking but the key'
to consummate the ages.

The Alchemy of Overcoming

Overcoming
the blackness
is the goal
of black loveliness
turning darkness
to light, for light
is blackness
made visible
as darkness
is brightness
transcended
by love.

Change – Schizophrenic

Expectation
clutches at sameness
while contradictorily searching
for stimulation

roads
must be predictable
beyond the next bend
yet predictability
is monotony
'round the bend'.

Does contradiction
extrapolate
a schizophrenic wish
to stand aloof
from decline,
embrace familiarity,
disregarding soul
and solar evolution?

Entropy rules
sidereal precession with
or without our consent.

Part 8

Turning, to a Modern Dreamtime

On the Cusp of Dreaming

Dreamed interacting
futures past
are a slow boat
encountering at Libra
the balance point's downward
and upward spiralled
images flicking
superimposing
held at the last
falling to a devourer
Sebek the Crocodile's
joints snapped inward
absorbing the trials
and 'Grapes of Wrath'
when destroyer and destroyed
appoint for themselves
on the upward way
one holding the vials
plagues and bounty alike

at the cusp of being
seeing and unseeing,
like the Barque of Ra.

Mangrove Swamp Evocation

Dark green bush dreams
clump together
like tough polished leaves
and twisted stems
groping
from wet sand reaches

surface piercing aerial roots
supplicate the breeze
suggesting decay
yet expecting
the next tide's
creek and beach running
saline draught

a coalescing power
processing poisons
in a halfway world
filtering
with predictable rhythms
a nursery of living forms.

At the Old Year's Edge

The long evening road
down-drops hill contours
to ageing caravans
bastardised into shacks
behind a sea wall

abbreviated days
disavow
fickle summer memories
withdrawn winter landscapes
seep quietness

trees stripped bare
endure razor-sharp winds,
reclaimed
bird deserted wetlands
are tickled
by their reed-taunted
long-breathed hiss.

A habitual stroller
defies seasonal cold
stick-tapping the bitumen
downhill
ignoring a back-slanted rise
shouldering
a shingle-banked sea front
stones through sand
like fruit in a Christmas cake
suddenly
soft sticky mud redeemed
by salt channel smell
tide wash and gull call.

Is it well
for yesterday's indefatigable
age-defying walker
at the old year's edge?

Aftermaths of Celebration

A bonfire's kicked ash
spun-spark remnants
briefly flaunt gold showers
before surrendering
to darkness.

Who can recall them
from aftermaths of celebration
when the last reveller departs
with slammed car doors
or over-the-limit footsteps?

Is memory
only in minds,
eye-tired glances
and anticlimactic sighs

afterwards?

Early Youth – Chasing Buses

I have stepped back in time
stopping the clock
for capricious afternoons
sideways
gravel-kicked tyre swirls
skidding across memory's tracks,
sibling cyclists rivalry
for a girl on a bus

cut corner races
falls
punctures
scar traced
quite unhelmeted tournaments
waged in her favour.

Does youth's road remember us?
I wonder.

Does she?

Two Breaths

Between two breaths
time is change
perception a range
of understood
half understood
misunderstood
or unperceived degrees
of unreality
the outcast mesh
netting love, hope, fear,
and eternally
surprisingly
fleeting intuitions
of joy, sorrow,
the absolute moment.

...and in Conclusion

Rembrandt's Vision

Truth is light
born out of darkness
the essential image
bare of ornament
the picture behind appearances
like the sun
behind the sun

self-portraits
among a plethora of faces
marked the passing of his time
each a furrowed presentation
of an age-eroding journey
from the unreal
to the real.

What did his Sabbath long
'Road to Emmaus' teach him;
did he, with 'the day far spent'
find at last
through common hospitality
the truth within the symbol?

Did he see
with those companions
when scarred hands broke the bread
that here within this little space
was the 'All within the All'
he had been seeking
all his days?

www.ingramcontent.com/pod-product-compliance
Lightning Source LLC
Chambersburg PA
CBHW070049120526
44589CB00034B/1677